math
expressions
Common Core

Dr. Karen C. Fuson

D1285537

Homework and Remembering Grade 1
Volume 2

This material is based upon work supported by the
National Science Foundation
under Grant Numbers
ESI-9816320, REC-9806020, and RED-935373.

Any opinions, findings, and conclusions, or recommendations expressed in this material
are those of the author and do not necessarily reflect the views of the National Science Foundation.

Name _____

Solve the story problem.

Show your work. Use drawings, numbers, or words.

1 9 zebras play. Then some more come to play. Now there are 13 zebras. How many zebras come to play?

zebras

☐ _____
　　　label

2 There are 12 pumpkins on the porch. 6 are small and the others are large. How many are large?

pumpkins

☐ _____
　　　label

3 Maya sees some ducks in a pond. 9 more ducks swim over. Now she sees 14 ducks. How many ducks did Maya see before?

pond

☐ _____
　　　label

Find the unknown partner.

4 $8 + \boxed{} = 12$　**5** $9 + \boxed{} = 16$　**6** $7 + \boxed{} = 15$

7 $6 + \boxed{} = 14$　**8** $5 + \boxed{} = 11$　**9** $6 + \boxed{} = 13$

Name _____

Subtract.

1   8
   − 5

2   6
   − 3

3   10
   − 1

4   9
   − 2

Find the unknown partner.

 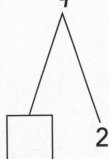 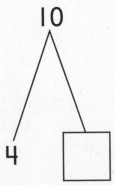 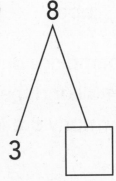 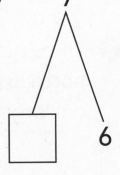

5   10
   4   ☐

6   9
   ☐   2

7   8
   3   ☐

8   7
   ☐   6

Count on to add.

9 $42 + 7 =$ ☐

10 $67 + 6 =$ ☐

11 $76 + 3 =$ ☐

12 $55 + 7 =$ ☐

13 ☐ $= 49 + 5$

14 ☐ $= 85 + 5$

15 **Stretch Your Thinking** I see some birds.

8 more birds come. Now I see 12 birds.

How many birds did I see before?

☐ birds

Unknown Partners with Teen Totals

Solve the story problem.

Show your work. Use drawings, numbers, or words.

---

1 14 apples are on a table. Then someone takes 6 of them. How many apples are on the table now?

table

[ ] _____
   label

---

2 12 toy trucks are on the floor. I put 3 of them away. How many toy trucks are still on the floor?

toy truck

[ ] _____
   label

Subtract. Use any method.

3 13 − 9 = [ ]   **4** 12 − 7 = [ ]   **5** 11 − 4 = [ ]

6 15 − 7 = [ ]   **7** 18 − 9 = [ ]   **8** 14 − 8 = [ ]

9 16 − 9 = [ ]   **10** 13 − 6 = [ ]   **11** 12 − 3 = [ ]

Write the partners and total for each circle drawing.

1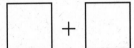

Total [ ]

2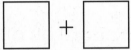

Total [ ]

Write the teen number.

3 ○ ○ [ ]

4 ○ ○ ○ ○ ○
○ ○ ○ [ ]

Solve the story problem.

Show your work. Use drawings, numbers, or words.

5 Emilio has a box of 10 pencils and 5 extra pencils. How many pencils does he have?

pencil

[ ] _____
label

6 **Stretch Your Thinking** Draw to show how to make a ten to subtract 15 − 8.

Subtraction with Teen Numbers

Solve the story problem.

Show your work. Use drawings, numbers, or words.

1 David makes 13 pots in art class. 5 of them break. How many pots are left?

pots

☐ _____
        label

2 16 bears are at a picnic. Some bears go home. 9 bears are still at the picnic. How many bears go home?

picnic

☐ _____
        label

3 We see 15 barns today. Some are red and some are white. How many red and white barns can there be? Show three answers.

barns

☐ red barns and ☐ white barns

or ☐ red barns and ☐ white barns

or ☐ red barns and ☐ white barns

Add.

4 $\begin{array}{r} 9 \\ + 4 \\ \hline \end{array}$ **5** $\begin{array}{r} 8 \\ + 9 \\ \hline \end{array}$ **6** $\begin{array}{r} 8 \\ + 6 \\ \hline \end{array}$ **7** $\begin{array}{r} 4 \\ + 9 \\ \hline \end{array}$

Name _____

Write how many.

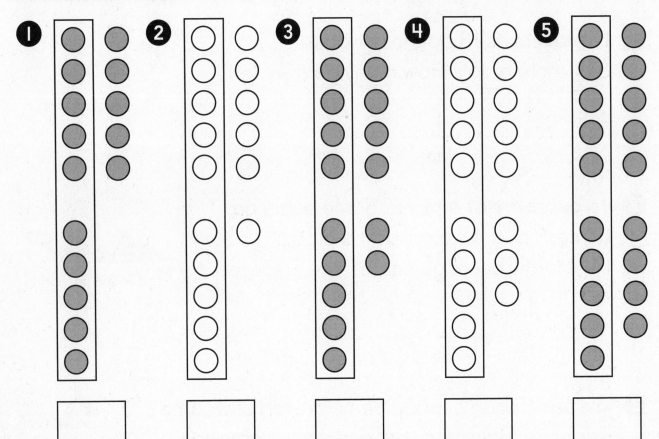

Subtract. Use any method.

6 14 − 7 = ☐   **7** 13 − 5 = ☐   **8** 15 − 7 = ☐

9 18 − 9 = ☐   **10** 15 − 8 = ☐   **11** 17 − 8 = ☐

12 **Stretch Your Thinking** Write a subtraction
story problem for a total of 14. Solve it.

_____

_____

Mixed Practice with Teen Problems

Solve the story problem.

Show your work. Use drawings, numbers, or words.

1 Hakim draws 8 stars. Lisa draws 7 stars. How many stars do they draw altogether?

star

☐ _____
label

2 There are 13 markers in a box. Jorge takes some out. Now there are 8 in the box. How many markers does Jorge take out of the box?

box

☐ _____
label

3 Karla plants 7 flowers. Then she plants 5 more flowers. How many flowers does Karla plant?

flower

☐ _____
label

Subtract.

4   16
     − 7
     ____

5   13
     − 5
     ____

6   15
     − 8
     ____

7   14
     − 9
     ____

Name _____

Find the total number of toys.

1 7 train cars in the box

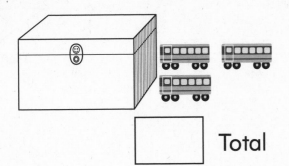

[ ] Total

2 5 bears in the box

[ ] Total

Add.

3 6 + 2 = [ ]

4 5 + 1 = [ ]

5 7 + 3 = [ ]

6 5 + 5 = [ ]

7 1 + 6 = [ ]

8 4 + 5 = [ ]

Show your work. Use drawings, numbers, or words.

Solve the story problem.

9 Stella picks 8 red flowers and 9 yellow flowers. How many flowers does she pick?

[ ] _____
label

flower

10 **Stretch Your Thinking** Noah makes a ten to solve Exercise 9. Draw to show how Noah solved the problem.

Small Group Practice with Teen Problems

Solve the story problem.

Show your work. Use drawings, numbers, or words.

1 Ted has 4 cousins that live in the city and 8 cousins that live on a farm. How many cousins does Ted have?

city

[   ] _____
label

2 Today, 9 geese land in our yard. Then 7 more geese come. How many geese are there?

goose

[   ] _____
label

3 A store has 13 jackets. Some jackets are sold. There are 8 left. How many jackets are sold?

jacket

[   ] _____
label

4 Nathan sees 16 windmills. Only 9 are spinning. How many windmills are not spinning?

windmill

[   ] _____
label

Name _____

Write the 10-partners and the switched partners.

1

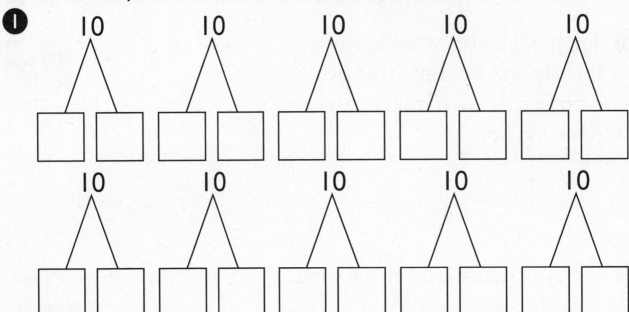

Count on to find the unknown partner.

2 4 + ☐ = 10   **3** 4 + ☐ = 9   **4** 3 + ☐ = 7

Show your work. Use drawings, numbers, or words.

Solve the story problem.

5 There are 7 ants on the leaf. Then 5 more ants come. How many ants are there in all?

☐ _____
      label

ant

6 Stretch Your Thinking Emma has 16 crackers. She eats some. Could she have 16 crackers left? Explain.

_____

_____

Teen Problems with Various Unknowns

Ring the 10-partners. Find the total.

1
       10
$7 + (2 + 8) =$ ☐

2
$3 + 7 + 9 =$ ☐

3
$6 + 5 + 5 =$ ☐

4
$4 + 6 + 5 =$ ☐

5
$9 + 1 + 6 =$ ☐

6
$8 + 7 + 2 =$ ☐

Solve the story problem.

Show your work. Use drawings, numbers, or words.

7 I draw 7 pictures of animals, 3 pictures
of people, and 6 pictures of houses.
How many pictures do I draw?

house

☐ _____
      label

8 I have 9 white marbles, 5 blue marbles,
and 3 green marbles. How many marbles
do I have in all?

marble

☐ _____
      label

Add 1 ten.

1 50 + 10 = ☐   **2** 80 + 10 = ☐

3 70 + 10 = ☐   **4** 30 + 10 = ☐

5 60 + 10 = ☐   **6** 40 + 10 = ☐

Write the next number.

7 | 38 | 39 | ☐ |

8 | 58 | 59 | ☐ |

9 | 78 | 79 | ☐ |

10 | 88 | 89 | ☐ |

Solve the story problem.

Show your work. Use drawings, numbers, or words.

11 8 cars are in the parking lot. Then 6 more cars come. How many cars are there now?

car

☐ _____
label

12 **Stretch Your Thinking** Look at the story problem in Exercise 11. What if 4 more cars come to the lot? How would you solve the problem?

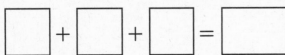
☐ + ☐ + ☐ = ☐

Problems with Three Addends

Color each 10-group a different color.
Count by tens and ones. Write the number.

1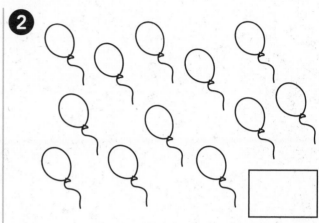

2

3

4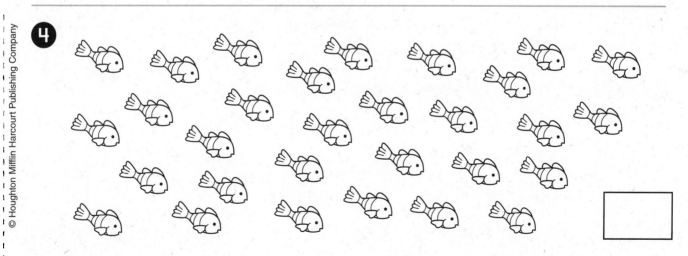

1 Write the numbers from 1–20.

I								
								19

Ring the 10-partners. Find the total.

2 (5 + 5) + 1 = [ ]   over the ring: 10

3 6 + 4 + 6 = [ ]

4 2 + 9 + 8 = [ ]

5 3 + 7 + 5 = [ ]

Add.

6 2 + 7 = [ ]

7 9 + 1 = [ ]

8 2 + 8 = [ ]

9 3 + 5 = [ ]

10 **Stretch Your Thinking** Draw 20 stars.
Ring the 10-groups.

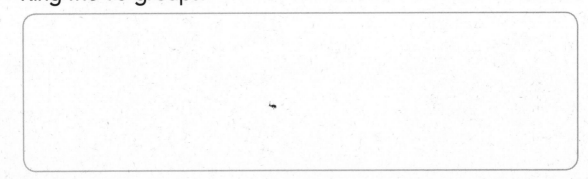

Count with Groups of 10

Number the houses in this town. Ring the number that is
10 more than 36. Cross out the number that is 10 less than 82.

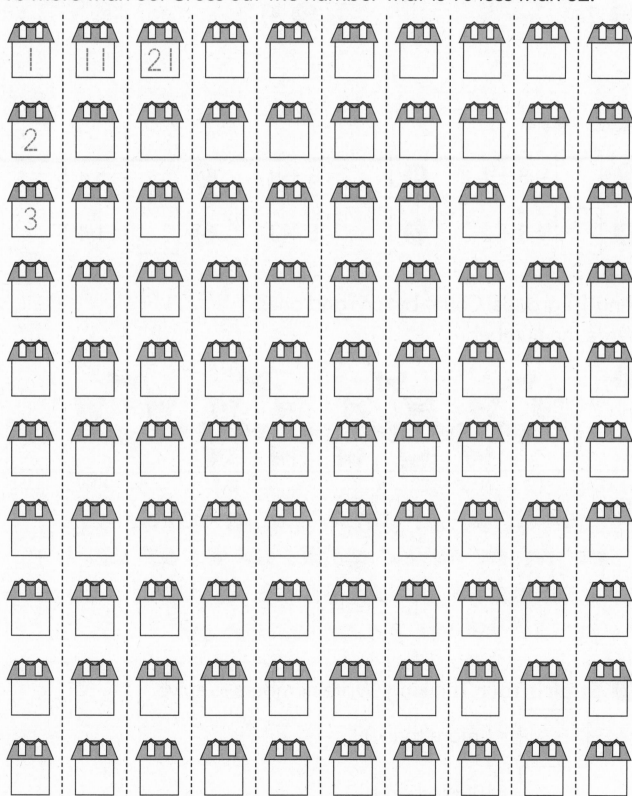

Draw 10-sticks and circles.

1 76

2 41

Add.

3 ☐ = 8 + 1   **4** ☐ = 3 + 4   **5** ☐ = 5 + 5

6 ☐ = 3 + 2   **7** ☐ = 5 + 3   **8** ☐ = 1 + 5

Ring 10-groups. Count by tens and ones.
Write the number.

9

☐

10

☐

11 **Stretch Your Thinking** Write numbers to solve.

☐ is 1 more than 99.

☐ is 10 less than 100.

Name _____

Continue the pattern.
Write the number that is 10 more.

1 | 22 | 32 | 42 | | | | |

2  19 29 39

3  48 58 68

Add tens.

4 52 + 10 = ☐   **5** 64 + 20 = ☐

6 15 + 60 = ☐   **7** 71 + 20 = ☐

Subtract tens.

8 40 − 10 = ☐   **9** 90 − 70 = ☐

10 80 − 30 = ☐   **11** 60 − 50 = ☐

12 70 − 50 = ☐   **13** 50 − 20 = ☐

Ring the 10-partners. Find the total.

1 $4 + 2 + 6 =$ ▭

2 $5 + 5 + 8 =$ ▭

3 $9 + 1 + 8 =$ ▭

4 $3 + 5 + 7 =$ ▭

Compare the numbers. Write <, >, or =.

5 28 ◯ 82

6 79 ◯ 80

7 36 ◯ 36

8 94 ◯ 94

9 32 ◯ 29

10 67 ◯ 63

Solve the story problem.

Show your work. Use drawings, numbers, or words.

11 Madison has a box of 10 crackers and 8 extra crackers. How many crackers does she have?

▭ _____
   label

cracker

12 **Stretch Your Thinking** Start at 48. Add 3 tens. Then add 4 ones. Draw to show your work. What is the number?

▭

Add and Subtract Tens

Solve.

1 20 + 80 = ☐

2 90 + 10 = ☐

3 30 + ☐ = 100

4 60 + ☐ = 100

5 100 = 50 + ☐

6 100 = 70 + ☐

---

7 40 + 30 = ☐

8 60 + 20 = ☐

9 0 + 90 = ☐

10 20 + 60 = ☐

---

11 70 − 20 = ☐

12 90 − 60 = ☐

13 20 − 0 = ☐

14 60 − 60 = ☐

---

15 80 − 30 = ☐

30 + ☐ = 80

16 90 − 20 = ☐

20 + ☐ = 90

17 80 − 50 = ☐

50 + ☐ = 80

18 70 − 30 = ☐

30 + ☐ = 70

Subtract.

1 10 − 8 = ☐   **2** 6 − 3 = ☐   **3** 9 − 8 = ☐

4   8   **5**   10   **6**   7
    − 5   − 6   − 5

Find the total. Use any method.

7 53 + 9 = ☐   **8** 75 + 2 = ☐

9 84 + 6 = ☐   **10** 39 + 4 = ☐

Continue the pattern.
Write the number that is 10 more.

11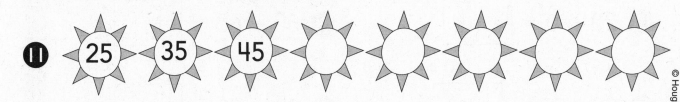
25 35 45

12 | 13 | 23 | 33 | | | | |

13 **Stretch Your Thinking**
Start with 50. Add 1 ten.
Then subtract 2 tens.
Draw to show your work.
What is the new number?

Add and Subtract Multiples of 10

Draw to show the numbers.
Write the numbers to solve.

Charlie gathers apples, pears, and plums.

- The numbers of apples and plums are 10-partners.

- There are the same number of apples and pears.

How many pieces of fruit could Charlie gather?

Apples	Pears	Plums

☐ apples + ☐ pears + ☐ plums = ?

☐ + ☐ = ☐ pieces of fruit

Write how many leaves. See the 5 in each row.

1 ☐	 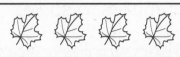
2 ☐	 
3 ☐	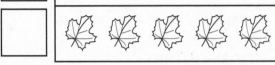

Solve.

4 $40 + \boxed{} = 100$

5 $70 + \boxed{} = 100$

6 $100 = 50 + \boxed{}$

7 $100 = 20 + \boxed{}$

8 $50 - 10 = \boxed{}$

9 $80 - 20 = \boxed{}$

10 $70 - 60 = \boxed{}$

11 $90 - 70 = \boxed{}$

12 **Stretch Your Thinking** Write and solve a story problem about gathering three kinds of vegetables. Use 10-partners.

_____

_____

_____

Focus on Mathematical Practices

1 Cut out the cards. Sort the creatures. Use circles and 5-groups to record. Write how many in each group.

Antennae	No Antennae

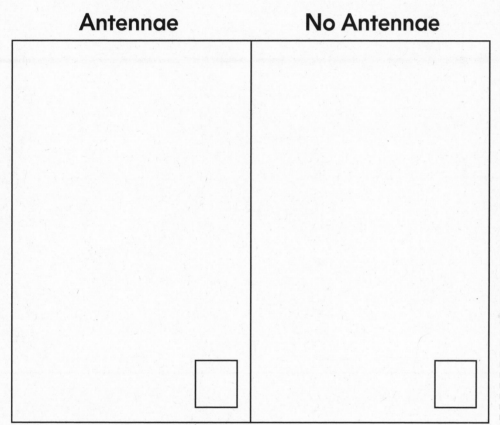

Use the data to complete.

2 How many creatures in all?

_____

3 Ring the group with more creatures.

4 Cross out the group with fewer creatures.

Explore Representing Data

Name _____

1 Write the numbers from 21–30.

Add.

2 $5 + 3 =$ ☐ **3** $2 + 7 =$ ☐ **4** $6 + 4 =$ ☐

5 $9 + 1 =$ ☐ **6** $3 + 4 =$ ☐ **7** $2 + 6 =$ ☐

Find the total.

8 $10 + 2 =$ ☐ **9** $10 + 3 =$ ☐

Solve the story problem.

Show your work. Use drawings, numbers, or words.

10 There are 8 birds on the fence. Then 7 more come. How many birds are there now?

fence

☐ _____
     label

11 **Stretch Your Thinking** Jen sorts a box of pens by color. 6 are red and 8 are blue. Draw circles and 5-groups to show how many in each group. Ring the group with more.

➡ **On the Back** Draw your answer on the back.

Name

© Houghton Mifflin Harcourt Publishing Company

1 Draw matching lines to compare.

Apple

Cherry

2 Complete the sentences.
Ring the word **more** or **fewer**.

There are ☐ **more fewer** apple pies than cherry pies.

There are ☐ **more fewer** cherry pies than apple pies.

3 Sort the balloons. Record with pictures.
Write how many in each group.

Gray Balloons							___
White Balloons							___

4 Complete the sentences. Ring the word **more** or **fewer**.

There are ☐ **more fewer** white balloons than gray balloons.

There are ☐ **more fewer** gray balloons than white balloons.

1 Write the numbers from 31–40.

Subtract.

2 $10 - 3 =$ ☐   **3** $9 - 7 =$ ☐   **4** $6 - 3 =$ ☐

5 $8 - 3 =$ ☐   **6** $10 - 4 =$ ☐   **7** $7 - 1 =$ ☐

Add I ten.

8 $30 + 10 =$ ☐

9 $50 + 10 =$ ☐

Solve the story problem.

Show your work. Use drawings, numbers, or words.

10 Pam sees 9 black cars. She sees 6 brown cars. How many cars does she see in all?

car

☐ _____
label

11 **Stretch Your Thinking** Draw circles and matching lines to show 9 flowers and 7 vases. Ring the extra flowers.

Organize Categorical Data

1 Kate runs 5 blocks. Ann runs 9 blocks.

Draw circles to show how many blocks they run.

Kate								
Ann								

2 Complete the sentences. Ring the word **more** or **fewer**.

Kate runs [ ] **more fewer** blocks than Ann.

Ann runs [ ] **more fewer** blocks than Kate.

They run [ ] blocks in all.

3 Dan does 4 jumps. Joel does 7 jumps.

Draw circles to show how many jumps they do.

Dan						
Joel						

4 Complete the sentences. Ring the word **more** or **fewer**.

Dan does [ ] **more fewer** jumps than Joel.

Joel does [ ] **more fewer** jumps than Dan.

They do [ ] jumps in all.

1 Write the numbers from 41–50.

Find the unknown partner.

2 $10 + \boxed{} = 12$ **3** $10 + \boxed{} = 14$

4 Draw matching lines to compare.
Complete the sentences below.
Ring the word **more** or **fewer**.

Houses

Birds

There are $\boxed{}$ **more fewer** houses than birds.

There are $\boxed{}$ **more fewer** birds than houses.

5 **Stretch Your Thinking** Juana draws 2 more houses in the picture above. Then she writes this sentence about it:
"There are 2 more houses than birds."
What is Juana's mistake?

_____

_____

Name _____

Use the data to answer the questions.

Buckets of Milk This Week

Molly	🪣	🪣	🪣	🪣	🪣	🪣	🪣	🪣	🪣	🪣
Greta	🪣	🪣	🪣	🪣	🪣					
Rosie	🪣	🪣	🪣	🪣	🪣	🪣	🪣	🪣		

1 Which cow gives the fewest buckets of milk? _____

2 Which cow gives 8 buckets of milk? _____

3 How many more buckets of milk does Molly
give than Greta? _____

Fish Caught at the Lake

Alonzo	🐟	🐟	🐟	🐟	🐟	🐟		
Dana	🐟	🐟	🐟	🐟	🐟	🐟	🐟	🐟
Ramona	🐟	🐟	🐟	🐟				

4 Who catches the most fish? _____

5 How many fewer fish does Ramona
catch than Dana? _____

6 How many fish are caught altogether? _____

Data Sets with Three Categories **141**

Name _____

1 Write the numbers from 51–60.

Find the total.

2 10 + 5 = ☐

3 10 + 7 = ☐

Show your work. Use drawings, numbers, or words.

Solve the story problem.

---

4 15 cups are on the shelf. Then Danni takes 9 of them. How many are on the shelf now?

cup

☐ _____
label

5 **Stretch Your Thinking** Write and answer a question about the data. Use **more** or **fewer**.

Bunny Jumps

Gray	
White	

_____

_____

Data Sets with Three Categories

Use the data to answer the questions.

Weather This Month

Sunny Days	☀ ☀ ☀ ☀ ☀ ☀ ☀ ☀ ☀
Cloudy Days	☁ ☁ ☁ ☁ ☁ ☁ ☁ ☁
Rainy Days	🌧 🌧 🌧 🌧 🌧

1 How many more sunny days
are there than rainy days? _____

2 How many fewer rainy days
are there than cloudy days? _____

3 How many cloudy days and rainy days are there in all? _____

Telephone Calls This Week

Nadia	📱 📱 📱 📱 📱
Julio	📱 📱 📱 📱 📱 📱 📱 📱 📱
Adam	📱 📱 📱 📱 📱 📱

4 Who makes the fewest telephone calls? _____

5 Who makes 6 telephone calls? _____

6 How many more calls does Adam
make than Nadia? _____

1 Write the numbers from 61–70.

Find the total.

2   6
     + 7

3   9
     + 5

4   8
     + 8

5   8
     + 4

6   5
     + 8

Solve the story problem.

Show your work. Use drawings, numbers, or words.

7 15 children are at a park. Some children go home. There are 8 children still at the park. How many children go home?

children

□ _____
   label

8 **Stretch Your Thinking** Write and answer a question about the data.

Bowls of Food Eaten this Week

 Fido

Champ

Rover

Data Collecting

Solve the story problem.
Use comparison bars.

Show your work.

---

1 Janeka draws 4 houses.
Kelly draws 3 more than
Janeka. How many houses
does Kelly draw?

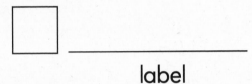

☐ _____
       label

---

2 Oak School has 9 computers.
Hill School has 4 computers.
How many fewer computers
does Hill School have than
Oak School?

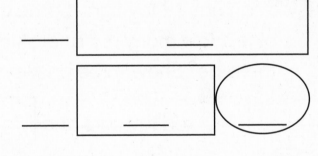

☐ _____
       label

---

3 Lisa makes 8 fewer pies than
Tony. Tony makes 14 pies.
How many pies does Lisa make?

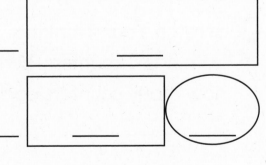

☐ _____
       label

Name _____

1 Write the numbers from 71–80.

Solve the story problem.

Show your work. Use drawings, numbers, or words.

2 I read 6 books last month. I read 6 books this week. How many books do I read in all?

book

☐ _____
label

3 Sean has 14 toy cars. Some are red. Some are blue. How many red and blue toy cars could there be? Show three answers.

☐ red toy cars and ☐ blue toy cars

or ☐ red toy cars and ☐ blue toy cars

or ☐ red toy cars and ☐ blue toy cars

4 **Stretch Your Thinking** Millie has 15 counters. Sam has 8 counters. Write a sentence comparing how many counters each child has.

_____

_____

Introduce Comparison Bars

Solve the story problem.
Use comparison bars.

Show your work.

1 Mike sees 3 more fish than
Chris. Chris sees 6 fish. How
many fish does Mike see?

[ ] _____
label

2 There are 10 fewer trumpets in
the band than drums. There are
20 drums. How many trumpets
are there?

[ ] _____
label

3 There are 9 girls and 15 boys
at the park. How many fewer
girls are there than boys?

[ ] _____
label

4 Kai ties 8 bows. Laura ties
13 bows. How many more
bows does Laura tie than Kai?

[ ] _____
label

Comparison Bars and Comparing Language **147**

1 Write the numbers from 81–90.

Use a double to find the total.

2 $6 + 8 =$ ☐　　**3** $5 + 7 =$ ☐　　**4** $5 + 6 =$ ☐

Solve the story problem.

Show your work. Use drawings, numbers, or words.

5 There are 14 muffins in a basket. Tina puts some on a plate. Now there are 6 in the basket. How many muffins does Tina put on the plate?

muffin

☐ _____
　　 label

6 **Stretch Your Thinking** Rewrite this sentence using the word **fewer**:
Carey reads 10 more pages than Lucey.

_____

_____

_____

Comparison Bars and Comparing Language

Solve the story problem.
Use comparison bars.

Show your work.

1 Toby has 12 balloons. Roberto
has 5 balloons. How many
more balloons does Toby have
than Roberto?

☐ _____

label

2 Nora has 4 candles on her cake.
Maria has 9 more candles than
Nora. How many candles does
Maria have?

☐ _____

label

3 Jordan hangs 15 flags. Alan
hangs 6 flags. How many
fewer flags does Alan hang
than Jordan?

☐ _____

label

1 Write the numbers from 91–100.

Draw 10-sticks and circles.

2 42

3 28

4 67

Solve the story problem.

Show your work. Use drawings, numbers, or words.

5 Ella paints 8 flower pots. Then she paints 4 more. How many flower pots does she paint?

[ ] _____
label

flower pot

6 **Stretch Your Thinking** Solve the story problem. Draw comparison bars.

Nathan has 9 fewer shells than Lidia. Lidia has 13 shells. How many shells does Nathan have?

[ ] _____
label

Solve *Compare* Problems

1 Sort the animals.
Record with circles and 5-groups.

Feathers	No Feathers

Use the data to complete.

2 How many more animals have feathers
than do not have feathers? _____

3 How many animals are there in all? _____

4 Write and answer your own question about
the data.

Name _____

Draw 10-sticks and circles.

1 53

2 82

3 94

Solve the story problem.

Show your work. Use drawings, numbers, or words.

4 A store has 15 guitars. Some guitars are sold. There are 9 guitars left. How many guitars are sold?

guitar

[   ] _____
label

5 **Stretch Your Thinking** Solve the story problem. Draw comparison bars.

There were 11 hikers here yesterday. There are 4 hikers here today. How many fewer hikers are here today than yesterday?

[   ] _____
label

Focus on Mathematical Practices

Name _____

Draw lines to match the time.

1  ———————— 2:00

2  3:00

3  6:00

4  5:00

5  10:00

1 Write the numbers from 101–120.

101	102	103						
111								

2 Draw matching lines to compare.
Complete the sentences. Ring the word **more** or **fewer**.

Dogs

Balls

There are ☐ **more fewer** dogs than balls.

There are ☐ **more fewer** balls than dogs.

Solve the story problem.

Show your work. Use drawings, numbers, or words.

3 Elena picks 7 red peppers and 8 yellow peppers. How many peppers does she pick?

pepper

☐ _____
label

4 **Stretch Your Thinking** It is 3 o'clock. Where does the hour hand point on an analog clock? _____

Introduction to Time

Read the clock.
Write the time on the digital clock.

1    7:00

hour : minute

2    :

hour : minute

3    :

4    :

5    :

6 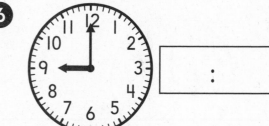   :

7 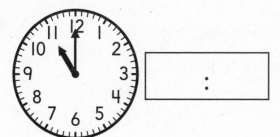   :

8    :

9 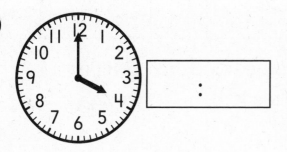   :

10 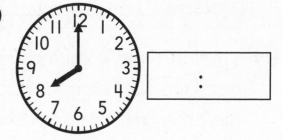   :

Subtract.

1 10 − 7 = ☐   **2** 9 − 5 = ☐   **3** 8 − 7 = ☐

4 9 − 9 = ☐   **5** 10 − 8 = ☐   **6** 7 − 2 = ☐

Draw lines to match the time.

7

☐ 8:00

8

☐ 5:00

9 Dave reads 7 books. Lani reads 9 books.
Draw ○ to show how many books they read.

Dave									
Lani									

10 **Stretch Your Thinking** The minute hand
points to 12. The hour hand points to 8.
Ring the time the clock shows.

8:00

12:00

Ring the clock that shows the correct time.
Cross out the clock that shows the wrong time.

1   11:00

2   2:00

3   5:00

4   3:00

5   10:00

6   9:00

7   8:00

8   1:00

Name _____

Write the next number.

1 | 58 | 59 | ___ | **2** | 38 | 39 | ___ |

3 | 88 | 89 | ___ | **4** | 68 | 69 | ___ |

Subtract. Use any method.

5 $17 - 9 = $ ☐   **6** $14 - 7 = $ ☐   **7** $13 - 6 = $ ☐

8 $16 - 7 = $ ☐   **9** $18 - 9 = $ ☐   **10** $12 - 8 = $ ☐

Read the clock. Write the time on the digital clock.

11
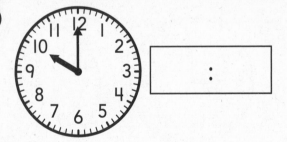
☐ : ☐

12
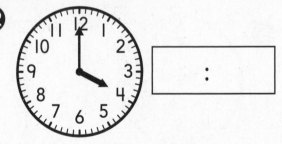
☐ : ☐

13 **Stretch Your Thinking** Tyrone says he eats
dinner when the minute hand is on 12. What
time do you think it is and why?

_____

_____

Time in Our Day

Read the clock.
Write the time on the digital clock.

1  | 8:30 |
hour : minute

2  | : |
hour : minute

3  | : |

4  | : |

5  | : |

6  | : |

7  | : |

8  | : |

9 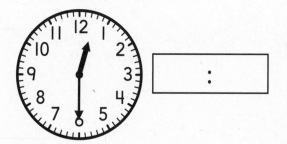 | : |

10  | : |

Name _____

Add.

1   8
   + 2

2   0
   + 7

3   3
   + 6

4   2
   + 2

5   1
   + 7

Use the data to answer the questions.

Muffins Baked for the Sale

Leon	
Shaw	
Rosa	

6 Who baked the most muffins? _____

7 Who baked 6 muffins? _____

Ring the clock that shows the correct time.
Cross out the clock that shows the wrong time.

8
6:00

9
3:00

10 **Stretch Your Thinking** What time
is a half-hour after 9:00? _____

Tell and Write Time in Half-Hours

Name _____

Write the time on the digital clock.

1

[:]

2

[:]

3

[:]

4

[:]

5

[:]

6

[:]

Draw the hands on the clock to show the time.

7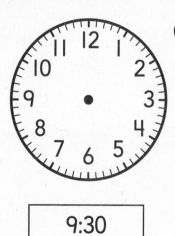

9:30

8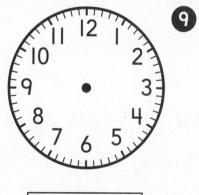

3:00

9

8:30

Name _____

Find the unknown partner.

① $4 + \boxed{} = 8$ | **②** $7 + \boxed{} = 10$ | **③** $5 + \boxed{} = 5$

Read the clock. Write the time on the digital clock.

④
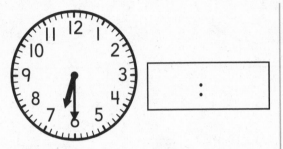

⑤
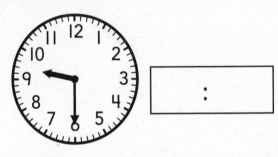

⑥
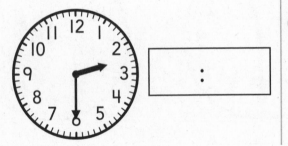

⑦

Show your work. Use drawings, numbers, or words.

Solve the story problem.

⑧ 16 hamsters are in the store.
8 are brown. The rest are white.
How many hamsters are white?

$\boxed{}$ _____
label

hamster

⑨ **Stretch Your Thinking** What are two
different ways to write four thirty?

Practice Telling and Writing Time

Name _____

1 Which shapes are NOT rectangles or squares?
Draw an X on each one.

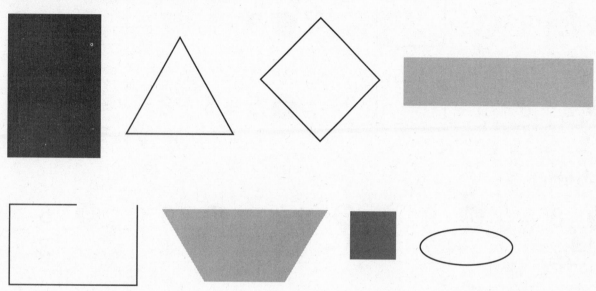

Draw the shape.

2 4 sides (2 long sides and 2 short sides), 4 square corners	**3** closed, 4 square corners

Squares and Other Rectangles **163**

Ring the 10-partners. Find the total.

1 ⑧+ 9 +② = [ ]   (over 8 and 2: 10)

2 9 + 1 + 7 = [ ]

3 2 + 8 + 5 = [ ]

4 5 + 5 + 8 = [ ]

Subtract.

5 8
− 2

6 9
− 7

7 6
− 6

8 10
− 1

9 5
− 3

Read the clock. Write the time on the digital clock.

10

[:]

11

[:]

12

[:]

13 **Stretch Your Thinking** Draw a shape with 4 sides and 4 corners that is not a rectangle. Explain your drawing.

_____

_____

Squares and Other Rectangles

Name _____

1 Which shapes are NOT triangles or circles?
Draw an X on each one.

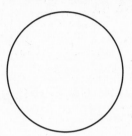 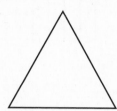

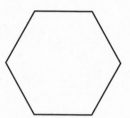   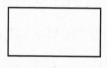

Draw the shape.

2 closed, no corners	**3** closed, 3 sides

Name _____

Write the number.

1 | | | | | | | | | | ○ ○ ○ ○ ⬜

2 | | | | | ○ ○ ○ ○ ○ / ○ ○ ○ ○ ⬜

Solve the story problem.

Show your work. Use drawings, numbers, or words.

3 There are 12 muffins in a box. Some are corn and some are berry. How many corn and berry muffins could there be? Show three answers.

muffin

⬜ corn muffins and ⬜ berry muffins

or ⬜ corn muffins and ⬜ berry muffins

or ⬜ corn muffins and ⬜ berry muffins

4 Which shapes are NOT rectangles or squares? Draw an X on each one.

 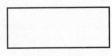

5 **Stretch Your Thinking** Draw two different triangles.

Triangles and Circles

Name _____

Draw a line to show halves.

    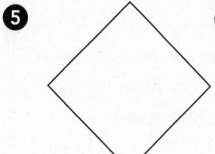   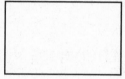

Draw lines to show fourths.

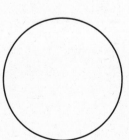   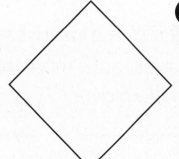

Name _____

Add.

① □ = 1 + 7   ② □ = 8 + 2   ③ □ = 3 + 6

④ □ = 5 + 5   ⑤ □ = 0 + 7   ⑥ □ = 1 + 4

Solve the story problem.

Show your work. Use drawings, numbers, or words.

⑦ There are 9 children on the bus. Then 5 more children get on. How many children are on the bus now?

bus

□ _____
   label

Draw the shape.

⑧ 4 sides, 4 square corners, closed

⑨ 3 sides, 3 corners, closed

⑩ **Stretch Your Thinking** Karim says he can fold a circle into halves more than 15 different ways. Is he correct? Explain.

_____

_____

Equal Shares

Draw a box around .

1 2 3

4

5 Tell your Homework Helper about these shapes.

Continue the pattern. Write the number that is 10 more.

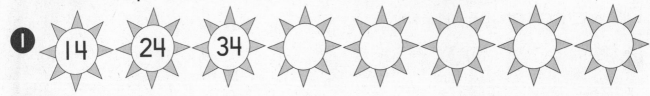

1 14 24 34

2 | 28 | 38 | 48 | | | | |

Solve the story problem.

Show your work. Use drawings, numbers, or words.

3 There are 8 bees in the hive. Some more bees come. Now there are 16 bees. How many bees come to the hive?

bee

_____
label

Draw a line to show halves.

4 　　**5**　　**6** 　　**7**

8 **Stretch Your Thinking** Can you make a rectangle with these squares? Draw to explain.

Compose 2-Dimensional Shapes

Name _____

Draw a line to match like shapes.
Write the name of the shape.

1   _____

2   _____

3   _____

4    _____

5   _____

Add.

1 8 + 2 = ☐   **2** 9 + 0 = ☐   **3** 6 + 1 = ☐

4 5 + 5 = ☐   **5** 2 + 4 = ☐   **6** 3 + 5 = ☐

Find the total. Use any method.

7 67 + 3 = ☐   **8** 85 + 6 = ☐

9 50 + 8 = ☐   **10** 77 + 5 = ☐

Draw lines to show fourths.

11   **12** **13** **14**

15 **Stretch Your Thinking** Name two objects in school that are shaped like a rectangular prism.

_____

_____

3-Dimensional Shapes

Name _____

Ring the shapes used to make the new shape.

1

2

3

4

Solve the story problem.

Show your work. Use drawings, numbers, or words.

1 There are 17 dogs in a store. Then 8 dogs are sold. How many dogs are left in the store?

☐ _____
    label

dog

Solve the story problem. Use comparison bars.

Show your work.

2 Ed has 10 bows. Kim has 3 bows. How many fewer bows does Kim have than Ed?

☐ _____
    label

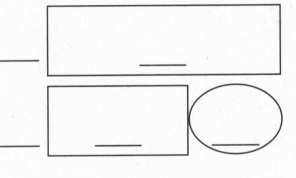

Draw a box around .

3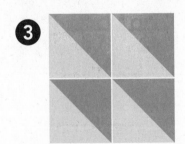

4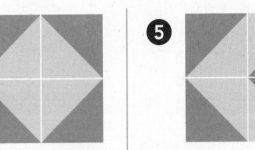

5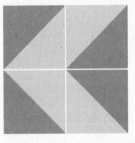

6 **Stretch Your Thinking** Sal wants to build a robot. He puts a sphere on top of a cylinder. What will probably happen?

_____

_____

Compose 3-Dimensional Shapes

① Write 1, 2, 3 to order from shortest to longest.

☐

☐

☐

② Write 1, 2, 3 to order from longest to shortest.

☐

☐

☐

Solve.

1 30 + ☐ = 100   **2** 80 + ☐ = 100

3 100 = 10 + ☐   **4** 100 = 40 + ☐

Solve. Watch the signs.

5 0 + 9 = ☐   **6** 7 + ☐ = 9   **7** ☐ + 0 = 8

8 7 − 4 = ☐   **9** 10 − ☐ = 7   **10** ☐ − 2 = 8

Draw a line to match like shapes.
Write the name of the shape.

Shape Names
sphere   cube   cone
cylinder   rectangular prism

11

_____

12

_____

13 **Stretch Your Thinking** Krystal puts three pencils in
order from longest to shortest. What is a fast way to
order the same pencils from shortest to longest?

_____

_____

Cut out the paper strips.
Measure the object in paper strips.

1 Pencil   How long? ☐ paper strips

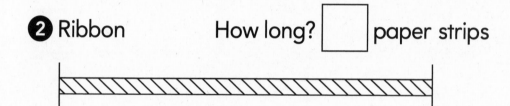

2 Ribbon   How long? ☐ paper strips

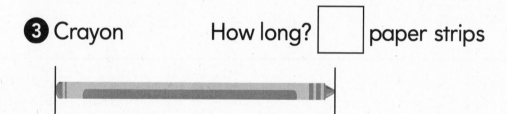

3 Crayon   How long? ☐ paper strips

4 Eraser   How long? ☐ paper strips

Measure with Length Units

Name _____

Solve the story problem. Use comparison bars.   *Show your work.*

1 There are 5 fewer pears
in the basket than apples.
There are 12 apples. How
many pears are there?

☐ _____
         label

2 Write 1, 2, 3 to order from shortest to longest.

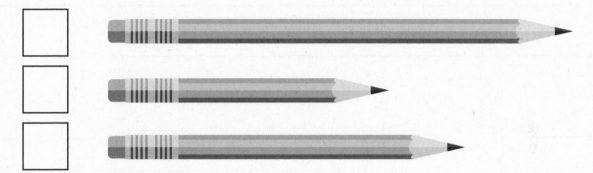

☐

☐

☐

3 Write the numbers from 101–120.

101	102	103							
111									

4 **Stretch Your Thinking** Aiden measures a book
with paper strips. It is actually 10 paper strips long,
but he gets an answer of 8. What is his mistake?

▶ **On the Back** Write or draw your answer on the back.

Name

Measure with Length Units

Name _____

1 Draw a square. Then draw a line to show halves.

_____

2 Draw a circle. Then draw lines to show fourths.

_____

Cut out the paper strips.
Measure the string in paper strips.

3 ⊢∿∿∿∿∿∿∿⊣   [ ] paper strips

4 ⊢∿∿∿∿∿∿∿∿∿∿∿∿∿⊣ [ ] paper strips

5 Draw a line longer than the string in Exercise 4.

Focus on Mathematical Practices

Solve the story problem.

Show your work. Use drawings, numbers, or words.

1 18 birds are in a tree. Some birds fly away. Now there are 9 birds in the tree. How many birds fly away?

bird

☐ _____
    label

Add.

2 ☐ = 4 + 6   **3** ☐ = 3 + 5   **4** ☐ = 0 + 9

Subtract.

5 7 − 7 = ☐   **6** 8 − 7 = ☐   **7** 10 − 0 = ☐

Find the unknown partner.

8 ☐ + 4 = 8   **9** ☐ + 6 = 9   **10** ☐ + 9 = 10

11 **Stretch Your Thinking** Leah and her 3 sisters want to share a pie. Draw lines to show how they can cut the pie into four equal shares.

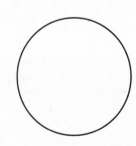

⬇ **On the Back** Draw 3 ribbons. Write 1, 2, 3 to order them by length from longest to shortest.

1 How many apples does Nick have?

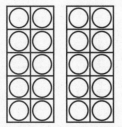

_____
label

2 How many apples does Sarah have?

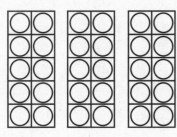 

_____
label

3 How many apples do Nick and Sarah have altogether?

Total

_____
label

Add the numbers with sticks and circles.

4
$$37$$
$$+\,46$$

Total

5
$$56$$
$$+\,28$$

Total

6
$$29$$
$$+\,63$$

Total

1 Write the numbers from 101–120.

Subtract.

2 $9 - 3 =$ ☐

3 $8 - 5 =$ ☐

4 $5 - 4 =$ ☐

5 $8 - 3 =$ ☐

6 $7 - 5 =$ ☐

7 $10 - 2 =$ ☐

Solve the story problem.

Show your work. Use drawings, numbers, or words.

8 Elena picks 6 apples. Ben picks some too. Together they pick 10 apples. How many apples does Ben pick?

apple

☐ _____
label

9 **Stretch Your Thinking** Sam drew sticks and circles to solve this problem. Explain how he added. Then write the total.

$$\begin{array}{r} 47 \\ + 33 \\ \hline \end{array}$$

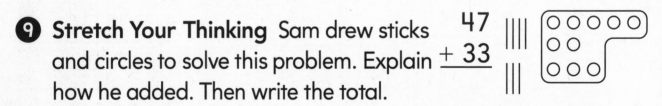

_____

_____

© Houghton Mifflin Harcourt Publishing Company

Explore 2-Digit Addition

Solve with numbers and with sticks and circles.

1   37
   + 45

2   16
   + 57

3   25
   + 39

4   81
   + 17

5   94
   + 5

6   48
   + 28

Name _____

Subtract.

1 7 − 3 = ☐   **2** 10 − 8 = ☐   **3** 5 − 2 = ☐

4   9
     − 3
─────

5   8
     − 5
─────

6   10
     − 9
─────

Use a double to find the total.

7 7 + 8 = ☐   **8** 5 + 6 = ☐   **9** 9 + 8 = ☐

Solve the story problem.

Show your work. Use drawings, numbers, or words.

10 We see 17 birds. Some are blue and some are black. How many blue and black birds can there be? Show three answers.

bird

☐ blue birds and ☐ black birds

or ☐ blue birds and ☐ black birds

or ☐ blue birds and ☐ black birds

11 **Stretch Your Thinking**
Write the numbers to match the sticks and circles. Then find the total.

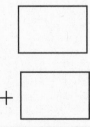

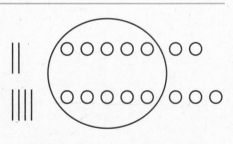

Methods of 2-Digit Addition

Name _____

Add. Make a Proof Drawing with sticks and circles.

1 67
+ 26

2 32
+ 37

3 38
+ 47

4 53
+ 39

5 How many nuts are there in all? Show your work.

48 nuts   48 nuts

┌─────────┐
│   │ _____
└─────────┘
       label

Add.

1 ☐ $= 5 + 3$ **2** ☐ $= 3 + 6$ **3** ☐ $= 6 + 4$

Solve.

4 $30 - 10 =$ ☐   **5** $60 - 30 =$ ☐

6 $10 - 10 =$ ☐   **7** $70 - 20 =$ ☐

Read the clock.

Write the time on the digital clock.

8
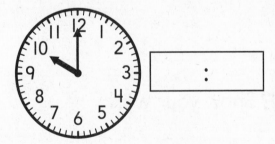

9
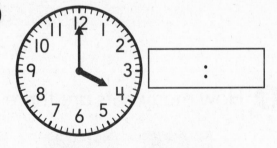

10 **Stretch Your Thinking** Don made this Proof Drawing to add $57 + 28$. He says the total is 75. What is Don's mistake?

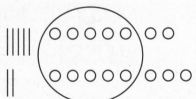

_____

_____

Addition of Tens and Ones

Name ______________________

Add. Make a Proof Drawing with sticks and circles.

1 $\begin{array}{r} 56 \\ +\ 28 \\ \hline \end{array}$	**2** $\begin{array}{r} 77 \\ +\ 21 \\ \hline \end{array}$
3 $\begin{array}{r} 47 \\ +\ 25 \\ \hline \end{array}$	**4** $\begin{array}{r} 34 \\ +\ 49 \\ \hline \end{array}$

Write the vertical form. Then add.

5 62 + 8	**6** 6 + 18

Name _____

Subtract.

1 8 − 4 = ☐   **2** 10 − 4 = ☐   **3** 9 − 4 = ☐

Solve the story problem.

Show your work. Use drawings, numbers, or words.

4 There are 15 muffins in a box. Lisa takes some out. Now there are 9 in the box. How many muffins does Lisa take out?

muffin

☐ _____
     label

Read the clock.
Write the time on the digital clock.

5

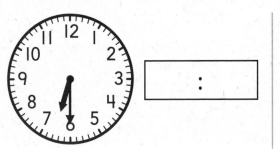

☐ : ☐

6

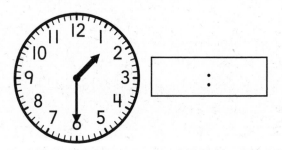

☐ : ☐

7 **Stretch Your Thinking** Will you make a new ten to solve this problem? Explain.

```
  59
+ 17
```

_____

_____

Discuss Solution Methods

Name _____

Add. Make a Proof Drawing with sticks and circles.

1
```
  28
+ 56
```

2
```
  16
+ 29
```

Write the vertical form. Then add.

3 16 + 3

4 58 + 20

How many peaches were picked by each pair? Show your work.

5
Carlos 16

Amy 39

6
Dora 49

Daniel 42

Name _____

1 Write the numbers from 101–120.

Solve the story problem.

Show your work. Use drawings, numbers, or words.

2 Kara has 8 shells. Sam gives her 8 more. How many shells does she have now?

shell

☐ _____
    label

Draw a line to show halves.

3

4

5 **Stretch Your Thinking** Is the total correct? Draw X if it is not correct. Write the correct total.

$$\begin{array}{r} 49 \\ + 33 \\ \hline 72 \end{array}$$

Practice 2-Digit Addition

Name _____

Use the pictures to solve.

1 How many apples are there?

[ ] apples

2 How many cartons of juice are there?

[ ] cartons of juice

3 Choose your own numbers between 10 and 49. How many jars of pickles are there?

[ ] jars of pickles

Solve.

1 30 − 10 = ☐

2 90 − 40 = ☐

Solve the story problem.

Show your work. Use drawings, numbers, or words.

3 A store has 15 lamps. 6 lamps are sold. How many lamps are in the store now?

☐ _____
    label

lamp

Write the vertical form. Then add.

4 42 + 9

5 53 + 7

6 **Stretch Your Thinking** Use the picture to write a math problem. Then solve.

_____

_____

_____

25 potatoes   38 potatoes

Focus on Mathematical Practices